Big Bear

Terry Barber

FIRST
NATIONS
SERIES

Big Bear is published by
Grass Roots Press, a division of Literacy Services of Canada Ltd.

PHONE: 1–888–303–3213
WEBSITE: www.grassrootsbooks.net

ACKNOWLEDGEMENTS

We acknowledge the financial support of the Government of Canada through the Canada Book Fund (CBF) for our publishing activities.

Produced with the assistance of
the Government of Alberta, Alberta
Multimedia Development Fund.

Alberta Government

Editor: Dr. Pat Campbell
Image research: Dr. Pat Campbell
Book design: Lara Minja, Lime Design Inc.

Library and Archives Canada Cataloguing in Publication

Barber, Terry, date
    Big Bear / Terry Barber.

(First Nations)
ISBN 978–1–77153–042–2 (pbk.)

    1. Big Bear (Cree chief). 2. Cree Indians—Kings and rulers—Biography. 3. Cree Indians—Prairie Provinces—Biography. 4. Readers for new literates. I. Title. II. Series: Barber, Terry, 1950– . First Nations

PE1126.N43B344 2014   428.6'2   C2014–906995–2

Printed in Canada.

Contents

Bison provide the Cree with meat,
clothes, tools, rope, and fuel.

The Bison

The bison run for their lives. Their feet beat the ground. Dust fills the air.

Millions of bison cover the land. The Cree people depend on the bison. Life is hard for the Cree. But the Cree are free.

The Cree make tools from the bisons' bones.

A Cree boy has a vision of the future.

Early Years

A Cree boy sees into the future.
He sees the coming of the white man.
He sees the loss of his people's land.
He sees a land without bison. The boy
does not like what he sees.

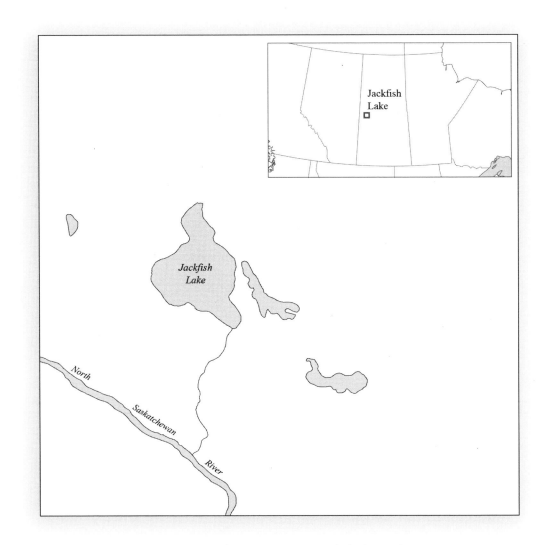

Big Bear is born near Jackfish Lake.

Today, Jackfish Lake is in Saskatchewan.

Early Years

The boy's name is Big Bear. He is born around 1825 near Jackfish Lake. His father is a Cree-Ojibwa chief. Big Bear is raised with the Plains Cree.

Big Bear learns to hunt bison.
He spends most of his time hunting.

The warriors return to their camp after a raid.

Early Years

As a young man, Big Bear becomes a warrior. The Blackfoot and Cree are enemies. The two tribes **raid** each other's camps. Big Bear steals horses from the Blackfoot tribe. He gives the horses to his people.

Big Bear is also called Mistahimaskwa.

Big Bear's camp.

Chief Big Bear

The year is 1865. Big Bear's father dies. Big Bear takes over as Chief. He is 40 years old.

The Cree people respect Big Bear. When Big Bear speaks, people listen. His voice is strong. His words are wise.

Big Bear's band has about 100 people.

Big Bear speaks to the white men at Fort Pitt.

Chief Big Bear

A white man calls Big Bear the best speaker he has ever heard.

In the white world, Big Bear could be a lawyer. He could be a politician. He could be anything he wants. But Big Bear is not part of that world.

The Battle of Belly River, 1870.

Chief Big Bear

In 1870, the Cree and the Blackfoot
go to battle. The Cree want the
Blackfoot's land. Over 500 men are
killed. Big Bear sees death all around
him. The Cree lose the battle. Big
Bear sees that violence cannot solve
problems.

The
Cree and the
Blackfoot sign
a peace treaty
in 1871.

A Cree woman, 1880.

A Time of Change

The 1870s is a time of great change.
Big Bear's childhood visions start
to come true. The white settlers are
taking over the land. They kill the
bison and sell the hides. The bison
herds grow smaller. Many Cree starve.

By the
1880s, the bison
are almost
gone.

Treaty 6 promises to give each band four oxen.

A Time of Change

The government wants the **Indians** to give up their land. The government wants the Cree to sign **Treaty** 6. The treaty makes many promises. The treaty promises food in times of hunger. The treaty promises that the Cree can choose their **reserve** land.

Treaty 6 promises to give farm tools and animals.

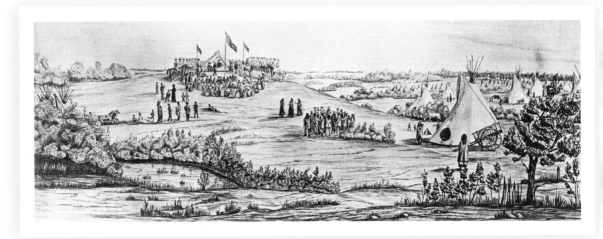

The Cree chiefs sign Treaty 6 at Fort Pitt.

Treaty 6

In 1876, most Cree chiefs sign Treaty 6. Those chiefs move their bands to reserves. The treaty promises to teach the Cree people how to farm.

Big Bear does not sign the treaty. Big Bear wants more rights for his people.

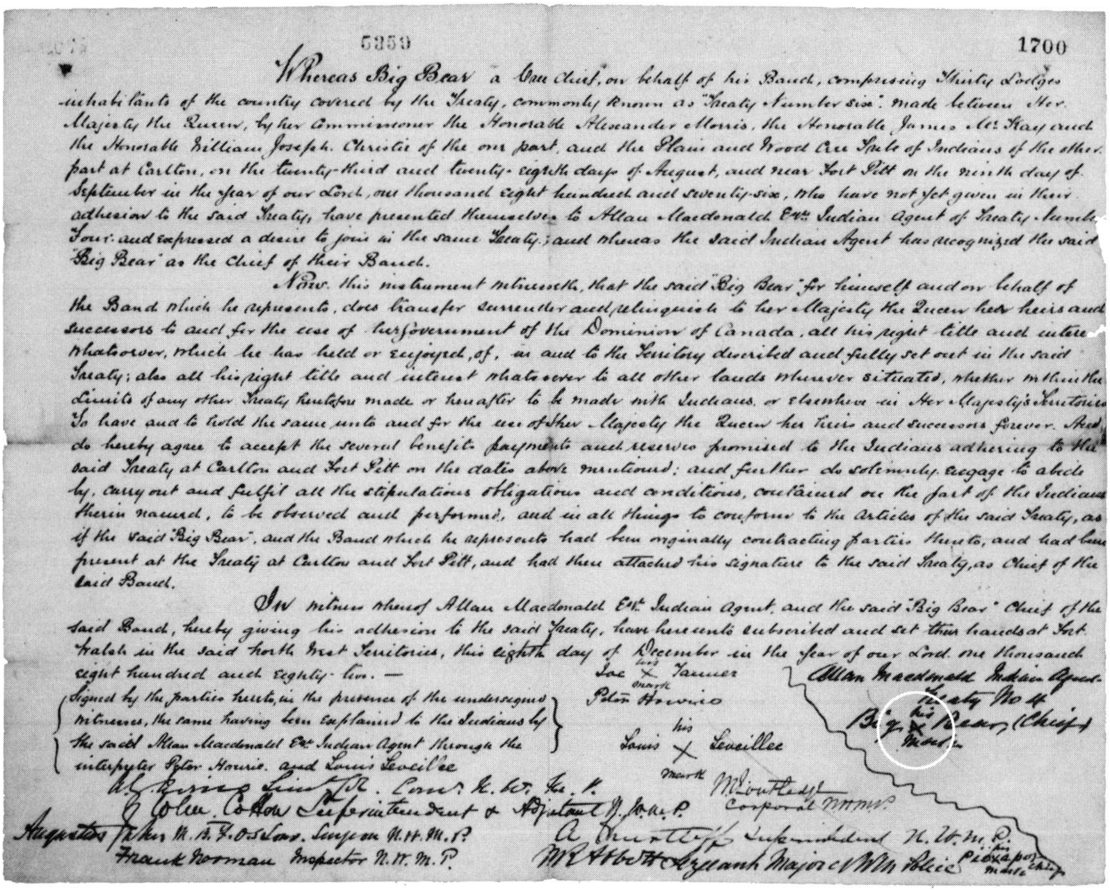

5359 1700

Whereas Big Bear a Cree chief, on behalf of his Band, comprising Thirty Lodges inhabitants of the country covered by the Treaty, commonly known as "Treaty Number six" made between Her Majesty the Queen, by her Commissioner the Honorable Alexander Morris, the Honorable James McKay and the Honorable William Joseph Christie of the one part, and the Plain and Wood Cree Tribe of Indians of the other part at Carlton, on the twenty-third and twenty-eighth days of August, and near Fort Pitt on the ninth day of September in the year of our Lord, one thousand eight hundred and seventy-six, who have not yet given in their adhesion to the said Treaty, have presented themselves to Allan Macdonald Esq. Indian Agent of Treaty Number Four: and expressed a desire to join in the same Treaty; and whereas the said Indian Agent has recognized the said "Big Bear" as the Chief of their Band.

Now this instrument witnesseth, that the said "Big Bear" for himself and on behalf of the Band which he represents, does transfer surrender and relinquish to her Majesty the Queen her heirs and successors to and for the use of her Government of the Dominion of Canada, all his right title and interest whatsoever, which he has held or enjoyed, of, in and to the Territory described and fully set out in the said Treaty; also all his right title and interest whatsoever to all other lands wherever situated, whether within the Limits of any other Treaty heretofore made or hereafter to be made with Indians, or elsewhere in Her Majesty's Territories To have and to hold the same unto and for the use of Her Majesty the Queen her heirs and successors forever. And do hereby agree to accept the several benefits payments and reserves promised to the Indians adhering to the said Treaty at Carlton and Fort Pitt on the dates above mentioned; and further do solemnly engage to abide by, carry out and fulfil all the stipulations obligations and conditions, contained on the part of the Indians therein named, to be observed and performed, and in all things to conform to the Articles of the said Treaty, as if the said "Big Bear", and the Band which he represents had been originally contracting parties thereto, and had been present at the Treaty at Carlton and Fort Pitt, and had there attached his signature to the said Treaty, as Chief of the said Band.

In witness whereof Allan Macdonald Esq. Indian Agent, and the said "Big Bear" Chief of the said Band, hereby giving his adhesion to the said Treaty, have hereunto subscribed and set their hands at Fort Walsh in the said North West Territories, this eighth day of December in the year of our Lord one thousand eight hundred and eighty-two. —

Signed by the parties hereto, in the presence of the undersigned witnesses, the same having been explained to the Indians by the said Allan Macdonald Esq. Indian Agent through the interpreter Peter Hourie and Louis Leveillee

Joe his X mark Tanner

Peter Hourie

Louis his X mark Leveillee

Allan Macdonald Indian Agent Treaty No 4

Big his X mark Bear (Chief)

[illegible] Lieut. [illegible] N.W.M.P.

[illegible] Cotton Superintendent & Adjutant N.W.M.P.

Augustus Jukes M.A. [illegible] Surgeon N.W.M.P.

Frank Norman Inspector N.W.M.P.

[illegible] Corporal N.W.M.P.

[illegible] Superintendent N.W.M.P.

[illegible] Sergeant Major N.W.M. Police

Piapot his mark Chief

Big Bear puts an "X" beside his name on Treaty 6.

Treaty 6

Many Indians do not like the treaty. They join Big Bear's band. His band grows in size. In 1882, Big Bear signs Treaty 6. He has little choice. The bison are gone. Big Bear's people have empty bellies.

By 1879, Big Bear's band grows to 2,000 members.

Cree people learn to farm.

Treaty 6

Farming is not easy. The soil is poor. Crops are hard to grow. The Indians still have empty bellies.

The government breaks its promises. The government does not provide enough food. Indians cannot choose their reserve land.

A Cree Thirst Dance.

Treaty 6

Time passes. Big Bear tries to unite the Cree bands. He wants one huge reserve for all Plains Cree.

Big Bear holds a Thirst Dance in 1884. The people pray, sing, and dance. And they talk about the treaty.

Over 2,000 Indians go to the Thirst Dance.

Louis Riel, 1884.

Louis Riel and Big Bear

Louis Riel is the **Métis** leader.
Riel wants more for his people, too.
He sends a list of demands to the
government. The government does not
meet the demands. Some of the Métis
decide to use force.

Queen Victoria.

Louis Riel and Big Bear

Big Bear meets with Riel. Big Bear says, "We should not fight the Queen with guns."

Big Bear wants to work with the white men. The white men have broken many treaty promises. Still, violence makes no sense to Big Bear.

The Queen of England represents Canada's government.

Wandering Spirit.

Broken Promises

Violence makes sense to some of Big Bear's band. The young Cree warriors plan an attack. They travel to Frog Lake on April 2, 1885. They raid the HBC store for food and supplies. The warriors hold some white settlers as **hostages**.

HBC is the Hudson's Bay Company.

Wandering Spirit kills a priest at Frog Lake.

Broken Promises

A warrior named Wandering Spirit takes control. He shoots one of the hostages. Big Bear hears the gunshot. He yells, "Stop, stop." The young warriors will not listen. Their anger comes from years of broken promises. They kill nine hostages.

The Frog Lake **massacre** is part of the **North-West Rebellion**.

Big Bear promotes peace at Fort Pitt, 1885.

Broken Promises

Two weeks pass. Wandering Spirit wants to capture Fort Pitt. He wants guns and supplies. Big Bear travels with the young warriors to Fort Pitt. Big Bear tries to stop more violence.

The warriors kill one white man at Fort Pitt.

Big Bear surrenders at Fort Carlton.

The Court Case

Big Bear surrenders on July 2, 1885. He is charged with **treason.** Witnesses say Big Bear did nothing wrong. Their words mean nothing. The white court wants to show the Indians who rules. Big Bear is found guilty of treason.

The court sentences Big Bear to three years in prison.

The Court Case

Big Bear has his say in court. He says: "I am old and ugly. But I have tried to do good. Pity the children of my tribe! Pity the old and helpless of my people. Big Bear has always been the friend of the white man."

Big Bear is released from prison in January 1887.

A Man of Peace

Big Bear spends over a year in prison.
In poor health, he is set free. Big Bear
dies on January 17, 1888.

The white man loses a friend.
The Indians lose a great leader.
Canada loses a man who believed
in peace.

Glossary

hostage: a person held prisoner until the captor's demands are met.

Indian: Indigenous people in Canada who are not Inuit or Métis. The term First Nations has replaced the word Indian.

massacre: the killing of many people in a violent way.

Métis: in the 1800s, Métis means a person of mixed Indian and European ancestry.

North-West Rebellion: a violent uprising led by Louis Riel against the Government of Canada.

raid: to attack suddenly.

reserve: land set aside by treaty for First Nations people.

treason: an act of betraying one's country.

treaty: an agreement between two or more nations.

Talking About the Book

What did you learn about Big Bear?

What did you learn about Treaty 6?

Do you think Big Bear was a warrior or a peacemaker? Explain your answer.

Do you think Big Bear was guilty of treason? Why or why not?

Picture Credits